20 Microwave Mug Cake Recipes

Perfect for that sweet craving when you only have a few minutes!

by
Jenny Scott

20 Microwave Mug Cake Recipes. Perfect for that sweet craving when you only have a few minutes!

Version 2014.08.21

Print Edition 1.1

ISBN : 978-1500910730

Introduction

The idea of a mug cake is that it is a single serving sweet treat that can be prepared with minimal effort and quite often with only a handful of ingredients.

Have you ever finished your meal and thought 'Gees I would love a cake or something sweet right now, but I have nothing prepared'? If so then mug cake recipes provide the prefect solution. Many of these recipes can be prepared in 5 minutes or less and require minimal effort to produce.

All the mug recipes in this book, have been created to be cooked in the microwave. The microwave used for these recipes has 1000W. You may find that you need to make slight adjustments to the timings of each recipe depending on your own microwave. This will not have an effect on the recipes just the times required to ensure that your delicious mug cakes are properly cooked.

There are a couple of considerations to bear in mind when choosing a suitable mug these recipes.

Firstly, you want a mug that will be safe to use in the microwave. So ideally you will have a ceramic mug that does not have any metallic designs or text on it. Basically a plain mug is the best way to go if possible.

Secondly, the size of the mug you will use. A standard mug has about 11 oz. (325 ml) capacity. When I mention a large mug this means that a mug of this size (11 oz.) or slightly bigger should be used. A number of the recipes will also work fine in a cup (8 oz. (227 ml) capacity).

Thirdly, the thickness of the cup will have an effect on how quickly the mug cake cooks. So if your mug is very thick then you will have to increase the times a little and obviously if your mug is very thin then you can reduce the microwave times a little.

Fourth and finally, when you remove your mug from the microwave it is always sensible to let it sit for 30 to 60 seconds before eating. This allows the heat to equalize and also should help prevent you from eating a cake that is too hot.

Sizing and Abbreviation

It makes sense that we just clarify the sizing and abbreviation used in this recipe book. Firstly, all of the recipes in this book are quoted first in imperial units with metric units in brackets.

Cup size can sometimes feel a bit ambiguous, so whenever a cup is referred to we are assuming a cup equals to 8 fluid ounces, which is approximately 227 ml.

A tablespoon, which has the abbreviation tbsp. in this book, is equal to half a fluid ounce, which equates to approximately 14 ml.

A teaspoon, which has the abbreviation tsp. in this book, is one sixth of a fluid ounce, which equates to approximately 5 ml.

All other abbreviations are standard, for example oz. for ounce, Kg for Kilogram.

Apple Cinnamon Mug Cake

This is a delightful mug cake recipe that is perfect for any occasion. If you don't have applesauce to hand you can substitute it for some finely shopped apple.

Ingredients for 1 Mug Cake

- 6 tbsp. All purpose flour
- 2 tbsp. Applesauce
- 2 tbsp. Brown Sugar
- 1 tbsp. Butter (melted)
- 1 tbsp. Milk
- 1 tsp. Ground Cinnamon
- ¼ tsp. Vanilla Extract
- ¼ tsp. Baking Powder

For the Icing

- 2 tbsp. Powdered Sugar
- 1 tbsp. Cream Cheese (ideally at room temperature)
- 1 tsp. Milk

Preparation – 7 to 10 minutes

1) Use a fork to whisk the icing ingredients together in a cup.

2) Set aside the icing.

3) In a mug mix together the flour, brown sugar, ground cinnamon and baking powder.

4) Add the applesauce to the mug and mix until combined so that you have a thick sticky mixture.

5) Add the vanilla extract, milk and butter to the mug and mix until moist (be careful not to over mix).

6) Place the mug in the microwave on high for 1 minute.

7) Remove the mug from the microwave and top with the set aside icing.

8) Serve and enjoy.

Chocolate Chip Brownie Mug Cake

This brownie makes fantastic company to those mid to late morning cups of coffee.

Ingredients for 1 Mug Cake

- 6 tbsp. All purpose flour
- 3 tbsp. Chocolate chips
- 3 tbsp. Brown Sugar
- 1 Egg (yolk only)
- 1 tbsp. Butter (melted)
- A pinch of Salt

Preparation – 4 to 6 minutes

1) Put the butter in a mug and melt in the microwave for 5 to 10 seconds.

2) Add the sugar, vanilla and pinch of salt to the melted butter and mix thoroughly.

3) Separate the egg yolk and egg white. Save the egg white for another recipe, it is not needed for this one.

4)   Add the flour and egg yolk to the mug and stir until completely combined. The mixture should be thick, if it is not add a little more flour until it is thick.

5)   Fold in the chocolate chips.

6)   Place the mug in the microwave for 30 seconds at 70% power. Before removing verify that the brownie is not wet on top. If it is wet microwave for a further 10 to 15 seconds at 70% power.

7)   Serve and enjoy.

Chocolate & Coffee Mug Cake

Everyone loves a chocolate sponge cake, and this is just the answer to that need.

Ingredients for 1 Mug Cake

- 6 tbsp. All purpose flour
- 4 tbsp. Sugar
- 4 tbsp. Milk
- 1 tbsp. Coffee (the stronger the better)
- 1 ½ tbsp. Cocoa powder (unsweetened)
- 1 tbsp. Vegetable Oil
- 1 tsp. Powder sugar (for dusting)
- ¼ tsp. Vanilla extract
- ½ tsp. Baking powder

Preparation – 4 to 6 minutes

1) In a mug thoroughly mix the flour, sugar, cocoa and baking powder together.

2) Add the coffee, vanilla extract, milk and oil to the mug and mix until combined. The mixture should be moist.

3) Put the mug in the microwave for 1 minute on full power. If the cake is wet on top return the microwave for a further 10 seconds.

4) Sprinkle the powder sugar on top of the cake.

5) Serve and enjoy.

Lime Coconut Mug Cake

Here is a fresh zesty tasting mug cake that is a real treat with a cup of tea or coffee. Suitable anytime of the day.

Ingredients for 1 Mug Cake

- 4 tbsp. All purpose flour

- 4 tbsp. Coconut Milk (full fat)

- 2 tbsp. Sugar

- 1 tsp. Coconut flakes

- ½ tsp. Lime Zest

- ¼ tsp. Baking powder

Preparation – 4 to 5 minutes

1) Mix together thoroughly in a Mug the flour, coconut milk, sugar and baking powder.

2) The mixture should be moist and smooth. Then quickly mix in half of the lime zest and all of the coconut flakes.

3) Place the mug in the microwave on full power for 1 minute. If the cake is wet return to the

microwave for a further 10 seconds.

4) Remove from the microwave and top with the remaining lime zest.

5) Serve and enjoy.

Chocolate Mug Cake

This a great cake to get the kids involved in making. Simple to make and very tasty, what more could you ask for?

Ingredients for 1 Mug Cake

- 4 tbsp. All purpose flour
- 3 tbsp. Vegetable oil
- 3 tbsp. Milk
- 2 tbsp. Cocoa powder
- 2 tbsp. Sugar
- 1 tbsp. Chocolate chips
- 1 Egg
- ¼ tsp. Vanilla extract

Preparation – 10 to 12 minutes

1)   Mix the flour, cocoa powder and sugar thoroughly in a mug.

2)   Break the egg and add it to the mug. Mix

thoroughly to ensure that all the flour is moist.

3) Add the vegetable oil, milk, vanilla extract and chocolate chips to the mug and mix thoroughly.

4) Place the mug in the microwave on full power for 3 minutes.

5) Remove the mug from the microwave and allow to set for 1 minute.

6) Serve and enjoy.

Nutella Mug Cake

For anybody else that cannot get enough of Nutella this is heavenly.

Ingredients for 1 Mug Cake

- 4 tbsp. All purpose flour
- 4 tbsp. Sugar
- 3 tbsp. Nutella
- 3 tbsp. Milk
- 3 tbsp. Cocoa powder
- 3 tbsp. Vegetable oil
- 1 Egg
- Pinch of Baking Soda

Preparation – 4 to 5 minutes

1) In a mug (large) mix thoroughly together the flour, sugar, cocoa powder and baking soda.

2) Beat the egg in a separate cup.

3) Add the vegetable oil and milk to the beaten egg and whisk together.

4) Pour the egg mixture into the cup with the flour. Add the Nutella also and mix thoroughly

together.

5) Place the mug in the microwave on full power for 2 minutes. If the cake is not fully cooked (use a fork to prick it and no flour should stick to the fork when it is removed) microwave for 10 seconds a time until cooked.

6) Serve and enjoy. A small dollop of vanilla ice cream goes great with this cake.

Cinnamon Roll Mug Cake

This is an absolute must if you are a cinnamon roll fan. This is a family favorite on Saturday mornings with a cup of coffee.

Ingredients for 1 Mug Cake

- 5 tbsp. All purpose flour
- 2 tbsp. Brown Sugar
- 2 tbsp. Applesauce
- 1 tbsp. Buttermilk
- 1 tbsp. Vegetable oil
- 1 tsp. Ground Cinnamon
- ¼ tsp. baking powder
- ¼ tsp. Vanilla Extract
- Pinch of Salt

Topping

- 2 tbsp. Powdered sugar
- 1 tbsp. Cream Cheese
- 1 tsp. Milk

Preparation – 3 to 5 minutes

1) In a mug (large) thoroughly mix together all of the ingredients for the cake.

2) Place the mug in the microwave on full power for 70 seconds. If the cake is not cooked (use a fork to prick it and no flour should stick to the fork when it is removed) microwave for a further 10 seconds and check again – repeat until cooked.

3) In a separate cup whisk together the topping ingredients until they form a smooth paste.

4) Cover the top of the cake with the topping.

5) Serve and enjoy.

Mug Cheesecake

This delicious mug cheesecake is so easy to make that you will quickly going back to make a second one.

Ingredients for 1 Mug Cake

- 4 tbsp. Cream Cheese
- 3 tbsp. Sugar
- 2 tbsp. Sour cream
- 1 Egg
- ½ tsp. Lemon Juice
- ¼ tsp. Vanilla Extract
- 4 Graham Crackers (crumbled)

Preparation – 4 to 5 minutes, plus 1 hour cooling time.

1) In a mug (large) thoroughly mix together the cream cheese, sugar, sour cream, lemon juice and the egg.

2) Place the mug in the microwave on full power for 30 seconds.

3) Remove the mug, stir it thoroughly and return to the microwave for a further 30 seconds on

full power.

4) Once again remove from the microwave and give a good stir before returning to the microwave for a further 30 seconds on full power.

5) Remove the mug from the microwave and sprinkle on the crumbled graham crackers.

6) Leave the mug to rest in a cool place for 1 hour.

7) Serve and Enjoy.

Chocolate Peanut Butter Mug Cake

This makes a great Sunday morning treat, either with a cup of coffee or in place of breakfast. No Mug cake recipe book would be complete without a peanut butter recipe.

Ingredients for 1 Mug Cake

- 3 tbsp. All purpose flour
- 3 tbsp. Milk
- 2 tbsp. Sugar
- 1 ½ tbsp. Vegetable Oil
- 1 ½ tbsp. Cocoa powder
- 1 tbsp. Peanut Butter
- ¼ tsp. Baking Powder
- Pinch of Salt

Preparation – 4 to 5 minutes

1) Whisk together thoroughly the flour, sugar, cocoa powder, baking powder and pinch of salt in a mug (large).

2) Stir in the milk, peanut butter and vegetable oil to the flour mix until the mixture has a smooth consistency.

3) Place the mug in the microwave for 1 minute 15 seconds on full power. Don't be shocked if the cake deflates quite a bit after it has risen, this is normal.

4) Serve and enjoy. A dollop of vanilla ice cream really tops this off nicely.

Banana Mug Cake

So simple, yet so good, this banana cake is very easy to make and requires very little effort. Tasty any time of the day, or night.

Ingredients for 1 Mug Cake

- 4 tbsp. Milk (almond milk if possible)
- 2 tbsp. All purpose flour
- ½ Banana (ripe)
- 1 tbsp. Nut butter
- 2 tsp. Sugar (Brown if possible)
- ¼ tsp. Baking powder

Preparation – 5 to 8 minutes

1) In a mug thoroughly mix together the flour and baking powder.

2) Add the milk and sugar to the mug and stir thoroughly until there are no lumps.

3) In a separate cup mash the half of a banana.

4) Add the mashed banana to the mug with the flour in it along with the nut butter and mix

thoroughly.

5) Place the mug in the microwave for 2 ½ minutes on full power. You may need to place for a few more seconds in the microwave if the cake comes out wet on top.

6) Remove from the microwave and serve. A dollop of ice cream or Chantilly goes nicely with this cake.

Chocolate Fudge Mug Cake

Here is one for those with really sweet teeth. This chocolate fudge mug cake is one you will find yourself making over and over again.

Ingredients for 1 Mug Cake

- 4 tbsp. All purpose flour
- 4 tbsp. Unsalted butter (melted)
- 3 tbsp. Graham crackers (crumbled)
- 2 tbsp. Cocoa powder
- 2 tbsp. Sugar
- 2 oz. (62 grams) Milk Chocolate Chips
- 1 Egg
- ½ tsp. Vanilla extract
- 1/8 tsp. Baking powder
- 4 Marshmallows
- Pinch of salt.

Preparation – 4 to 7 minutes

1)   In a small bowl mix together 3 tbsp. of melted

butter with half of chocolate chips.

2) Place the small bowl in the microwave on full power for 30 seconds so that the chocolate chips have melted.

3) In a mug mix together the graham crackers crumbs with the remaining 1 tbsp. of melted butter. Push down firmly on this mixture so that it is in the bottom of the mug.

4) In a separate bowl mix together thoroughly the sugar, egg and vanilla extra until it forms a smooth paste.

5) Add the flour, cocoa, salt and baking powder to the bowl with the egg mixture and stir until it forms a consistent batter.

6) Add the chocolate chip butter batter and mix thoroughly before stirring in the remaining half of the chocolate chips.

7) Put half of this flour batter directly on top of the grahams crackers, followed by 3 marshmallows, before adding the rest of the flour batter.

8) Place the mug in the microwave on full power for 1 minute 45 seconds.

9) Place the remaining marshmallow on top of the cup and microwave for a further 10 seconds.

10) Serve and enjoy.

Blueberry Mug Cake

Who doesn't love blueberry muffins? This mug cake replaces the need for all that effort to prepare one muffin. The sponge is not exactly like that of a muffin, but it tastes so good you will not care.

Ingredients for 1 Mug Cake

- 4 tbsp. All purpose flour
- 4 tbsp. White Sugar
- 3 tbsp. Vegetable oil
- 3 ½ tbsp. Milk
- 8 Blueberries (fresh)
- 1 Egg
- ½ tsp. Baking powder
- ¼ tsp. Vanilla Extract

Preparation – 4 to 5 minutes

1) In a mug (large) mix together thoroughly the flour, sugar and baking powder.

2) In a separate cup or small bowl whisk together

the egg with the oil, milk and vanilla extract.

3)   Add the egg mixture to the flour mixture and combine thoroughly so that all of the flour is moist.

4)   Add the blueberries to the mug.

5)   Place the mug in the microwave for 1 minute 40 seconds on full power. You may need to place for a few more seconds in the microwave if the cake comes out wet on top.

6)   Serve and Enjoy. Note a dollop of fresh cream makes a great addition to this cake.

Rich Lemon Mug Cake

This is a fresh lemon tasting cake with a mild zesty kick. It is simply delicious.

Ingredients for 1 Mug Cake

- 4 tbsp. All purpose flour
- 3 tbsp. Milk
- 1 tbsp. Lemon Curd
- ½ tbsp. Vegetable Oil
- 2 tsp. White Sugar
- 1 tsp. Lemon Zest
- ¼ tsp. Vanilla Extract
- ¼ tsp. Baking powder.

Preparation – 4 to 5 minutes

1) In a mug (large) mix thoroughly together the flour, sugar and baking powder.

2) Add the milk, vegetable oil, and vanilla extract to the flour mixture and whisk together until a smooth batter is formed.

3) Add the lemon curd and lemon zest to the mug

and mix thoroughly.

4)   Place the mug in the microwave for 60 to 70 seconds on full power. You may need to place for a few more seconds in the microwave if the cake comes out wet on top.

5)   Serve and Enjoy.

Peach Cobbler Mug Cake

An autumn favorite for the whole family.
Perfect for those cool evenings.

Ingredients for 1 Mug Cake

- 2 tbsp. All purpose flour
- 2 tbsp. Sugar
- 2 tbsp. Milk
- 1 tbsp. Butter
- 1 Peach – peeled and sliced.
- 1/8 tsp. Cinnamon
- 1/8 tsp. Baking Powder

Preparation – 4 to 5 minutes

1) Place the butter in the bottom of a mug and microwave for 10 seconds (just enough to melt the butter).

2) Add the flour, milk, sugar, cinnamon and baking powder to the mug with the melted butter and stir thoroughly making sure that the mixture is smooth and moist.

3) Rest the peach slices to the top of the mug

without mixing them with the batter.

4)   Place the mug in the microwave on 80% power for 2 minutes.

5)   Serve and enjoy. Note that a dollop of vanilla ice cream is excellent with this cake.

Apple Pie Mug Cake

Not strictly a cake, but I could not leave this delightful recipe out of this book. A true American classic ready in a matter of minutes.

Ingredients for 1 Mug Cake

- 2 cups chopped apple – cored and skinned.
- 2 to 3 plain cookies – crumbled
- 1 ½ tsp. Butter
- 1 tsp. All purpose flour
- 1 tsp. Powdered sugar
- ¼ tsp. Cinnamon powder
- Pinch of salt
- Pinch of grated nutmeg
- A dollop of ice cream or whipped cream

Preparation – 5 to 7 minutes

1) Make sure that the apple has been chopped into small chunks.

2) Place the chopped apples, butter, flour,

cinnamon powder, grated nutmeg, pinch of salt and sugar into a mug.

3)   Combine the mixture so that the apples are covered with a touch of all the ingredients.

4)   Place the mug in the microwave of full power for 2 minutes 15 seconds.

5)   Remove the mug from the microwave and top with the crumbled cookies.

6)   Add the dollop of ice cream (vanilla has to be the best) or whipped cream to the top of the mug.

7)   Serve and enjoy.

Pineapple Upside Down Mug Cake

For the pineapple lovers out there this upside down cake is perfect.

Ingredients for 1 Mug Cake

- 3 tbsp. Brown Sugar
- 2 tbsp. All purpose flour
- 2 tbsp. Crushed pineapple
- 2 tbsp. Butter
- 2 tbsp. Milk
- 1 Egg
- ¼ tsp. Baking Powder
- Pinch of Salt

Preparation – 7 to 10 minutes

1) Mix together the pineapple, 2 tbsp. of sugar and 1 tbsp. of butter in a mug (large).

2) Place the mug in the microwave of full power for 1 minute.

3) In a separate cup or small bowl cream together the remaining 1 tbsp. of butter with the remaining 1 tbsp. of sugar.

4) Separate the egg white from the yolk. Only the egg white is needed for this recipe.

5) In another cup or small bowl mix together the flour, milk, egg white baking powder and pinch of salt.

6) Combine the creamed butter with the flour mixture and then place on top of the pineapple in the mug.

7) Place the mug in the microwave on full power for 1 minute.

8) Remove the mug from the microwave and flip the cake out onto a place.

9) Serve and enjoy.

Bailey's Mug Cake (Alcoholic)

For those that like a spiked cake this Bailey's mug cake is just the treat you have been waiting for. Not for children though!

Ingredients for 1 Mug Cake

- 6 tbsp. All purpose flour
- 4 tbsp. Sugar
- 3 tbsp. Vegetable Oil
- 3 tbsp. Bailey's Irish Cream Liquor
- 1 Egg
- ¼ tsp. Baking powder

Preparation – 4 to 5 minutes

1) In a mug (large) thoroughly mix together the flour, sugar, and baking powder.

2) In a separate cup or small bowl beat the egg and whisk together with the vegetable oil and Bailey's.

3) Add the egg mixture to the flour mix and whisk together until the mixture is moist.

4) Place the mug in the microwave for 1 minute 45 seconds on full power. You may need to place for a few more seconds in the microwave if the cake comes out wet on top.

5) Serve and enjoy.

Spicy Ginger Coffee Mug Cake

Here is a tasty treat that mixes the spicy ginger with a kick of coffee. Be sure to try this one out.

Ingredients for 1 Mug Cake

- 5 tbsp. All purpose flour
- 4 tbsp. Sugar
- 3 tbsp. Milk
- 3 tbsp. Vegetable oil
- 2 tbsp. Strong coffee (brewed)
- 1 tbsp. Molasses
- ¼ tsp. Ground Cinnamon
- ¼ tsp. Ground Ginger
- ¼ tsp. Baking powder
- 1 Egg

Preparation – 5 to 6 minutes

1) In a large mug mix together the flour, sugar, molasses, cinnamon, ginger and baking powder.

2) In a separate cup or small bowl beat the egg and

then whisk in the milk, coffee and vegetable oil.

3) Add the egg mixture to the flour mixture and combine until completely moist.

4) Place the mug in the microwave on full power for 1 minute 45 seconds. You may need to place for a few more seconds in the microwave if the cake comes out wet on top.

5) Remove from the microwave, serve and enjoy. Note that a dollop of whipped cream on top goes down a treat with this cake.

Coffee Walnut Mug Cake

Here is nutty Walnut cake that is washed down well with a cup of coffee.

Ingredients for 1 Mug Cake

- 6 tbsp. Non-fat plain Yogurt
- 5 tbsp. All Purpose Flour
- 5 tbsp. Honey
- A small handful of crushed Walnuts
- ½ tsp. Coffee (Brewed ideally)

Preparation – 5 to 8 minutes

1) In a small bowl mix together the honey and the plain yogurt.

2) Add the flour to the bowl and mix thoroughly until you have a dough.

3) Add the crushed walnuts and the coffee to the bowl and mix in.

4) Pour the contents of the bowl into a mug.

5) Place the mug in the microwave on full power for 4 minutes 30 seconds. You may need to place for a few more seconds in the microwave

if the cake comes out wet on top.

6) Remove the mug from the microwave and allow to cool for one minute before serving.

7) Serve and enjoy.

Avocado Mug Cake

This light fluffy mild taste is pleasant treat anytime of the day.

Ingredients for 1 Mug Cake

- 4 tbsp. All purpose flour
- 4 tbsp. Sugar
- 4 tbsp. Milk
- Half an Avocado (ripe)
- ¼ tsp. Baking powder

Preparation – 4 to 5 minutes

1) Mash the avocado into a pulp in a mug (large).

2) Add the flour, sugar, milk and baking powder to the mug with the avocado and mix thoroughly until you have a smooth batter.

3) Place the mug in the microwave on full power for 2 minutes. You may need to place for a few more seconds in the microwave if the cake comes out wet on top.

4) Serve and enjoy.

38247322R00028

Printed in Great Britain
by Amazon